SHIFTER KARTS:
HIGH-SPEED GO-KARTS

by Matt Doeden

Reading Consultant:
Barbara J. Fox
Reading Specialist
North Carolina State University

Capstone press

Mankato, Minnesota

Blazers is published by Capstone Press,
151 Good Counsel Drive, P.O. Box 669, Mankato, Minnesota 56002.
www.capstonepress.com

Library of Congress Cataloging-in-Publication Data
Doeden, Matt.
    Shifter karts : high-speed go-karts / by Matt Doeden.
    p. cm.—(Blazers: horsepower)
    Includes bibliographical references and index.
    ISBN 0-7368-3790-6 (hardcover)
    1. Karting—Juvenile literature. I. Title. II. Series.
GV1029.5.D64 2005
796.7'6—dc22   2004018538

Summary: Discusses shifter karts, their main features, and how
    they are raced.

Editorial Credits
Erika L. Shores, editor; Jason Knudson, set designer; Patrick D.
    Dentinger, book designer; Wanda Winch, photo researcher;
    Scott Thoms, photo editor

Photo Credits
Bill Kistler, 4–5, 6–7, 8–9, 10–11, 12–13, 16, 18–19, 20–21, 22–23, 28–29
Jayne Oncea, cover, 14–15, 17, 22, 24–25
Jim Coppage, 26–27

1 2 3 4 5 6 10 09 08 07 06 05

TABLE OF CONTENTS

SHIFTER KARTS

The whine of 20 powerful
go-kart engines fills the air.
The karts speed away as the
race begins.

Number 29 jumps out to an
early lead. The driver leans into the
turns. He shifts gears to go faster
down straightaways.

On the last lap, number 70 passes the leader. The driver speeds through one more turn and wins the race.

KART DESIGN

Shifter karts are small go-karts. They are the fastest kind of go-kart.

Shifter karts have small, smooth tires called slicks. The tires grip the tracks to help drivers make high-speed turns.

BLAZER FACT

Most kart races are 12 to 15 laps long. A kart takes about 30 seconds to complete one lap.

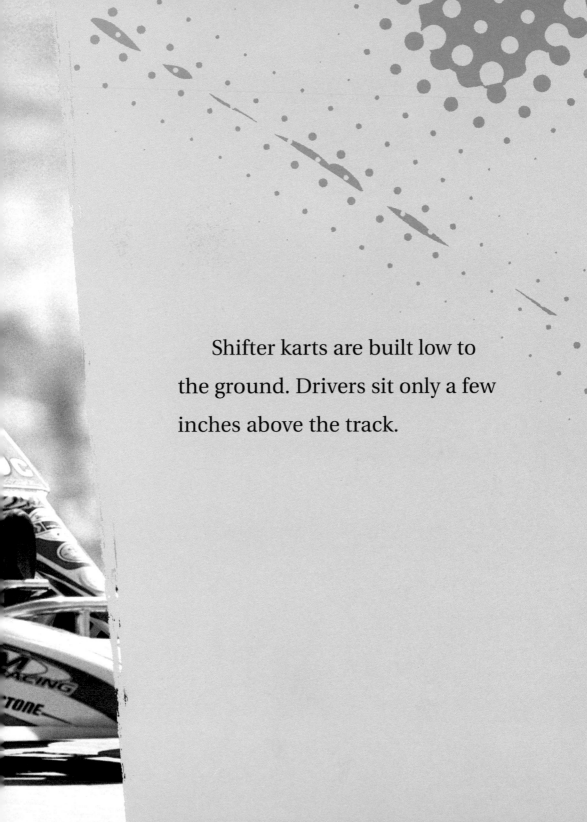

Shifter karts are built low to the ground. Drivers sit only a few inches above the track.

Shifter karts have motorcycle
engines. Karts can go more than 100
miles (160 kilometers) per hour. Drivers
shift through six gears as they go faster.

BLAZER FACT

Many famous drivers, including Jeff Gordon and Sam Hornish Jr., raced go-karts.

Engine

Slick

18

Steering wheel

Nose piece

Shifter

SAFETY

Safety is important to shifter kart drivers. They wear helmets, gloves, and racing suits.

Shifter karts often spin out or crash. Many tracks have stacks of tires or hay bales. They stop karts from spinning off the track.

Spin out

SHIFTER KARTS IN ACTION

Kids and adults race shifter karts. Drivers race against people in their age group.

Shifter kart drivers race on smooth tracks. Some tracks are ovals. Other tracks have many twists and turns.

BLAZER FACT

The first go-karts were modeled after soapbox derby cars.

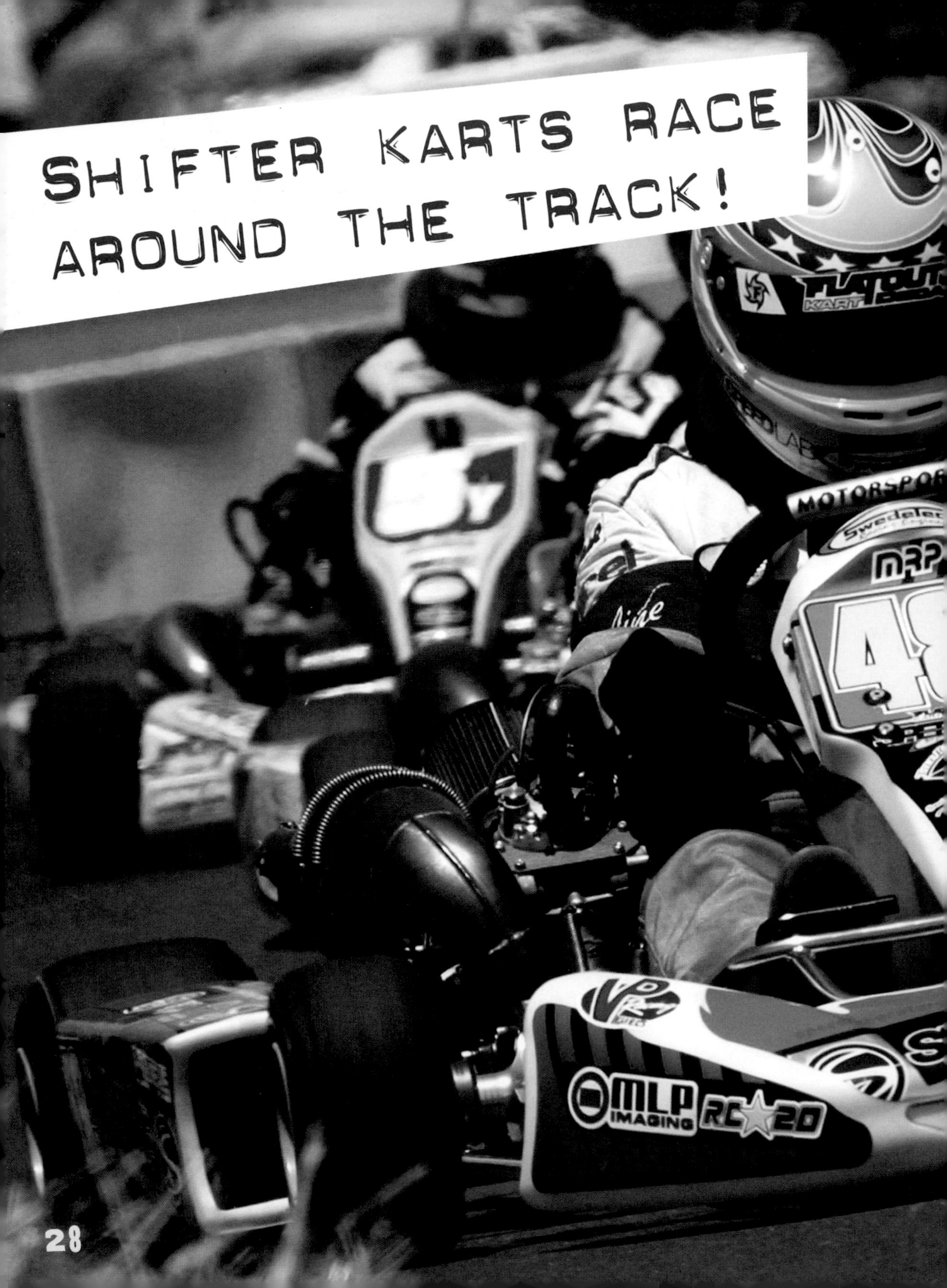

SHIFTER KARTS RACE AROUND THE TRACK!

GLOSSARY

gear (GIHR)—a set of wheels with teeth that carry an engine's power to the axles

lean (LEEN)—to shift one's body weight into a turn

oval (OH-vuhl)—an elongated circle

shift (SHIFT)—to change gears

slick (SLIK)—a soft, smooth tire used on go-kart racetracks

spin out (SPIN OUT)—to make a vehicle's rear tires lose grip, causing the vehicle to spin

straightaway (STRAYT-uh-way)—a long, straight part of a track

READ MORE

Herran, Joe, and Ron Thomas. *Karting*. Action Sports. Philadelphia: Chelsea House, 2004.

Martin, Gary. *Go Kart Racing—Just for Kids: A Step by Step Guide to Go Kart Racing*. Ft. Wayne, Ind.: Martin Motorsports, 2000.

Savage, Jeff. *Go-Karts*. Wild Rides! Mankato, Minn.: Capstone Press, 2003.

INTERNET SITES

FactHound offers a safe, fun way to find Internet sites related to this book. All of the sites on FactHound have been researched by our staff.

Here's how:

1.Visit *www.facthound.com*
2. Type in this special code **0736837906** for age-appropriate sites. Or, enter a search word related to this book for a more general search.
3. Click on the **Fetch It** button.

FactHound will fetch the best sites for you!

INDEX